MYSTERIES IN HISTORY
WILLIAM KIDD'S LOST TREASURE

by Becca Becker

Ideas for Parents and Teachers

Pogo Books let children practice reading informational text while introducing them to nonfiction features such as headings, labels, sidebars, maps, and diagrams, as well as a table of contents, glossary, and index.

Carefully leveled text with a strong photo match offers early fluent readers the support they need to succeed.

Before Reading

- "Walk" through the book and point out the various nonfiction features. Ask the student what purpose each feature serves.
- Look at the glossary together. Read and discuss the words.

During Reading

- Have the child read the book independently.
- Invite them to list questions that arise from reading.

After Reading

- Discuss the child's questions. Talk about how they might find answers to those questions.
- Prompt the child to think more. Ask: How much did you know about pirates before reading this book? Where would you bury treasure?

Pogo Books are published by Jump!
3500 American Blvd W, Suite 150
Bloomington, MN 55431
www.jumplibrary.com

Copyright © 2026 Jump!
International copyright reserved in all countries.
No part of this book may be reproduced in any form without written permission from the publisher.

Jump! is a division of FlutterBee Education Group.

Library of Congress Cataloging-in-Publication Data is available at www.loc.gov or upon request from the publisher.

ISBN: 979-8-89213-804-8 (hardcover)
ISBN: 979-8-89213-805-5 (paperback)
ISBN: 979-8-89213-806-2 (ebook)

Editor: Katie Chanez
Designer: Molly Ballanger

Photo Credits: Fer Gregory/Shutterstock, cover (treasure); MIGUEL G. SAAVEDRA/Shutterstock, cover (paper); powerofforever/iStock, cover (portrait); Sergej Razvodovskij/Shutterstock, 1; Kunz Husum/Adobe Stock, 3; Karl Allen Lugmayer/Adobe Stock, 4; James Thornhill/Wikimedia, 5; The Picture Art Collection/Alamy, 6-7; Bettmann/Getty, 8-9; durmus1986/Shutterstock, 10 (left); Image Asset Management/World History Archive/SuperStock, 10 (right); 19th era/Alamy, 11; GreenTree/Shutterstock, 12-13 (silk); RHJPhtotos/Shutterstock, 12-13 (iron); S_Photo/Shutterstock, 12-13 (background); API/Gamma-Rapho/Getty, 14-15; Patrick Guenette/Dreamstime, 15; Mary Evans Picture Library/Pantheon/SuperStock, 16; Amerigo_images/Shutterstock, 16-17 (background); North Wind Picture Archives/Alamy, 18; Egor_Kulinich/Shutterstock, 19; gary corbett/Alamy, 20-21; Jay Yuan/Shutterstock, 23.

Printed in the United States of America at Corporate Graphics in North Mankato, Minnesota.

TABLE OF CONTENTS

CHAPTER 1
Sailing the Seas 4

CHAPTER 2
Turning Pirate 10

CHAPTER 3
Long Lost Treasure 18

QUICK FACTS & TOOLS
Map and Quick Facts 22
Glossary 23
Index 24
To Learn More 24

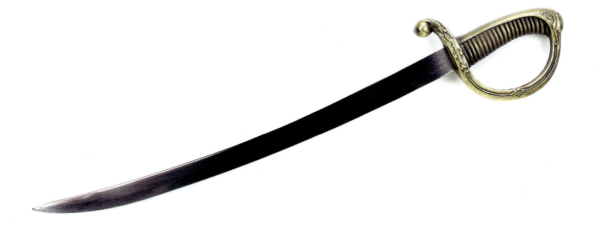

CHAPTER 1
SAILING THE SEAS

William Kidd was born in 1645. He grew up in Scotland. He loved the sea. He worked on ships.

William Kidd

In 1689, **Captain** Kidd was a **privateer** for England. The English government paid Kidd. His job was to attack enemy ships.

CHAPTER 1 5

Kidd had many adventures. Like what? He sailed North America's East Coast. He sailed in the Caribbean Sea, too. Kidd and his **crew** stole **cargo** from French ships. They gave it to England.

DID YOU KNOW?

England and France were at war in the late 1600s. Privateers from both sides attacked and stole from each other.

CHAPTER 1

CHAPTER 1

Kidd

CHAPTER 1

In 1696, Kidd and his crew sailed to the Indian Ocean. They were sent to attack enemy ships and **pirates**. They only got paid if they **captured** ships. That hadn't happened in months. Kidd's crew grew angry. The men fought with Kidd. They said they would take over the ship if things didn't change.

WHAT DO YOU THINK?

Kidd's ship was named *Adventure Galley*. A galley is a ship with oars. That means the ship can be rowed. If you had a ship, what would you name it? Why?

CHAPTER 1

CHAPTER 2
TURNING PIRATE

Kidd and his crew began stealing **treasure** from any ship they saw. Many of the ships were owned by the Mughal **Empire**. It ruled much of India.

The Mughals were important trading partners with England. England's leaders were angry with Kidd.

In 1698, a large ship called *Quedagh Merchant* sailed in the Indian Ocean. Its captain was English. Kidd wasn't allowed to attack the ship. He did anyway. He stole silk, iron, sugar, and more. The cargo would be worth $2.5 million today. It was a huge prize for Kidd's crew. England's leaders called Kidd a pirate. They wanted him arrested.

CHAPTER 2

CHAPTER 2

Kidd knew he was in trouble. He went to the Caribbean. He got a new ship. Why? He hoped it would help him hide. He also had friends in North America. One was Richard Coote. He was the governor of the New York and Massachusetts **colonies**. Kidd hoped Coote would help him. He set sail for Boston, Massachusetts.

Richard Coote

On his way, Kidd buried his treasure. Why? He did not want the English government to get it. He buried some on Gardiners Island. Kidd left gold, silver, and jewels.

When Kidd got to Boston, Coote had him arrested. Kidd went to England for his **trial**. He was found **guilty** of piracy.

TAKE A LOOK!

Where did Kidd sail on his way to Boston? Take a look!

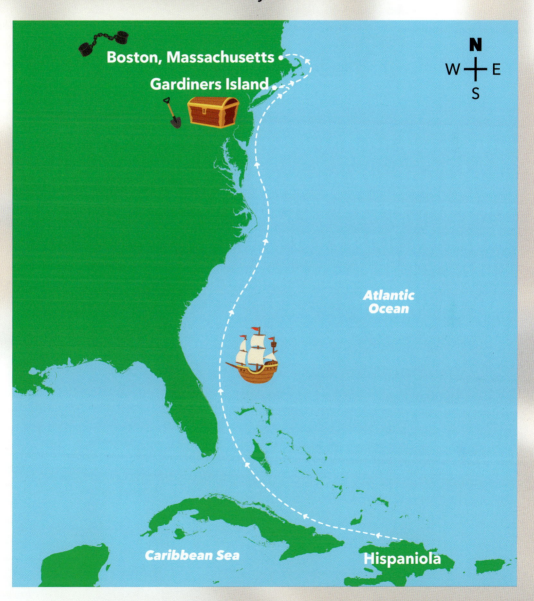

CHAPTER 2

CHAPTER 3

LONG LOST TREASURE

Kidd said he buried more treasure. But he would not say where. People have looked for it for years. They look along the East Coast. Why? Kidd sailed there on his way to Boston.

One popular searching spot is Charles Island in Connecticut. People walk the beach and search. They use **metal detectors**. They hope to find treasure buried under the sand. As of early 2025, none had been found.

metal detector

CHAPTER 3   19

Oak Island is near Nova Scotia, Canada. Treasure hunters look here, too. They have spent millions of dollars searching. They use big machines to dig up the island. They also have not found anything. No one knows where Kidd's treasure is. But many people want to find it!

WHAT DO YOU THINK?

The location of Kidd's treasure is a mystery. Where would you search for it? Why?

CHAPTER 3

QUICK FACTS & TOOLS

WILLIAM KIDD'S LOST TREASURE

QUICK FACTS

Who: Captain William Kidd

Crime: Piracy

Buried Treasure Locations: Gardiners Island, possibly other spots on North America's East Coast, and on islands in the Caribbean Sea

GLOSSARY

captain: The person in charge of a ship.

captured: Taken by force.

cargo: Items that are carried by a ship.

colonies: Areas that have been settled by people from another country and are controlled by that country.

crew: People who work on a ship.

empire: A group of countries or states that have the same ruler.

guilty: Responsible for a crime.

metal detectors: Devices that detect, or spot, hidden metal like gold.

pirates: People who attack and rob ships.

privateer: A sailor who attacks enemy ships for the government.

treasure: Gold, jewels, money, or other valuable things that have been collected or hidden.

trial: The examination of evidence in a court of law to decide if a charge is true.

QUICK FACTS & TOOLS

INDEX

Adventure Galley 9
arrested 12, 16
Boston, Massachusetts 15, 16, 17, 18
cargo 6, 12
Caribbean Sea 6, 15, 17
Charles Island 19
colonies 15
Coote, Richard 15, 16
crew 6, 9, 10, 12
England 5, 6, 11, 12, 16
France 6
Gardiners Island 16, 17

Indian Ocean 9, 12
metal detectors 19
Mughal Empire 10, 11
Oak Island 20
pirates 9, 12
privateer 5, 6
Quedagh Merchant 12
Scotland 4
stole 6, 10, 12
trading partners 11
treasure 10, 16, 18, 19, 20
trial 16

TO LEARN MORE

Finding more information is as easy as 1, 2, 3.

1. Go to www.factsurfer.com
2. Enter "WilliamKidd'slosttreasure" into the search box.
3. Choose your book to see a list of websites.

QUICK FACTS & TOOLS